Letters to My Sister

Simple Thoughts for a Complex World

By Deborah Cort

Copyright © 2012 by Deborah Cort

Letters to My Sister
Simple Thoughts for a Complex World

Printed in the United States of America
ISBN 978-0-9832-399-4-9
All rights are reserved solely by the author. The author declares that the contents are original and do not infringe on the rights of any other person.

No part of this book may be reproduced in any form except with permission from the author.
The views in this book are not necessarily the views of the publisher.

Scripture are taken from the Holy Bible, New International Version®, NIV®. Copyright © 1973, 1978, 1984, 2011 by Biblica, Inc.™ Used by permission of Zondervan. All rights reserved worldwide.
www.zondervan.com.

Letters to My Sister

Having a Mary Heart in A Martha World
Joanna Weaver
Published by Waterbrook Press
Copyright 2000

Seven Things That Steal Your Joy
Joyce Meyer
Published by Time Warner Book Group
Copyright 2004

Letters to My Sister

ACKNOWLEDGEMENTS AND SPECIAL THANKS

It is important to me that I acknowledge and say thank you to the special people in my life that have either been on this journey with me or who have influenced my life in a tremendous way.

First and foremost I want to and need to thank and acknowledge my Lord Jesus Christ who has never and will never give up on me. Even during a period in my life where I did not trust Him or almost did not even believe in Him, He never left me alone. Jesus has comforted me and guided me during all the bumpy paths that I have been on during my life. He has given me my life back and He is showing me who I am to be through Him.

The Lord has blessed me even when I did not know what a blessing was. He continues to grow my mind, grow my heart and grow my spirit. He has given me a phenomenally talented, wise, kind and generous husband and three incredibly beautiful, sweet, smart and entertaining children. The Lord has been so good to me, even when I did not deserve it.

I need to acknowledge and thank the only man in my life, who like God, really does love me unconditionally. My husband has seen the good the bad and the ugly in me but he never stopped loving me and he has never stopped believing in me. He is a powerful and wise man of God who walks the talk.

He is sold out to God and Gods purpose in his life. He is a tremendous father and father figure not just to our children but to others as well. He is a man of integrity, truth and love. I am honored, humbled and blessed to call him my husband. Thank you Sean for being a husband who is committed to me and our family and someone who is loving, kind and generous. I love you more than words can say.

My daughter Chanel has taught me so much about being me. The words that come out of her mouth and the expressions she uses to get her point across are strikingly similar to mine. During low times in my life, she has been the reason why I know I must go on. Watching her grow up (and grow up fast) is an absolute joy and she inspires me to be a better person each and every day. God knew what He was doing when he gave me this little girl. I am so proud of all that you have accomplished in your life and I am eagerly awaiting your God ordained future. Thank you Chanel for always being My Sunshine, always wanting a hug and always being the most perfect daughter for me. I love you. XXOO

My son Christian is a gentle kind soul who is growing up to be an incredible gentleman. He reminds me to relax and have fun and look at things simply instead of making things so complicated in my mind. He too, is growing up so fast but during his growth physically, mentally and spiritually he is becoming a son every mother wish they had. Thank you Christian for always being there with a kind word, a gentle hug or even a teasing word. Your love for me and this family comes out in everything that you do. I love you dearly.

Letters to My Sister

Aaron, the youngest, is such a delight to have around the house. He is the child who asks a million questions and is always interested in hearing your answer. He is the boy who is always smiling and his smile really does light up the whole room. You can't have a bad day when Aaron is around. I truly enjoy watching him grow and learn each and every day. His sense of humor makes me laugh even when I may not feel like it. Thank you Aaron for your kindness, your gentleness, your patience and your love. I love you baby.

I want to acknowledge my sister, Melissa, who has put up with me for so many years. Even though I tortured you for many years (scaring you by dangling you over the balcony, riding with me on a bike on gravel with no shoes on and no brakes, sitting through many a fashion show before I went out on a date and tickling you till you peed your pants) I know you would always be there for me.

Even though I wrote this book for all of "my sisters" out there, I hope this book specifically touches your heart and eventually the heart of your daughter, my niece. Through this book, I pray that you continue to see the need for the Lord in your life and that you continue to grow in your relationship with Him. I love you now and always.

My mom has been one of the strongest influences in my life. Her untimely death has still left a hole in my heart. I always say my 30th year of life was the best year of my life and the worst year of my life all rolled into one. That is the year I lost my mom but also the year my daughter was born. I try not to live with too many regrets in my life but one regret I do have is that my new best friend (my daughter) did not get to meet my old best friend (my mom). Mom, thank you for always pushing me and encouraging me to do the best in everything that I do. All of my successes is because of you and what you taught me. I don't think you ever anticipated me writing a book. But here it is. I think you would be proud. Oh and yes, I do have one more regret, mom I should have told you more how much I love you.

I also want to thank you dad, for bringing home the bacon and providing for your family. Thank you dad for your encouragement as well as for listening to me and giving me advice when I needed it. Thank you for your continuous love even when I did not deserve it. Pray this book blesses you too. Just know I do love you.

And finally, I want to acknowledge and thank the many women who have embraced me and encouraged me during these last few years. For some reason, I have not had a lot of close girlfriends over the years. This is probably because I had lost trust in friendship with women. I want to thank all
of you for showing me that there are women out there who are sincere, trustworthy and real.

I sincerely hope and pray that this book is a blessing to you all. Thank you for your support.

INTRODUCTION

Several years ago, when I seriously began my journey with the Lord, I dedicated myself to reading many Christian books along with the Bible. As I began my reading, the Lord kept telling me to write down in a small notecard all the meaningful scriptures as well as all the meaningful text that I would come along on my journey. I did not really understand why at first but as I went along and had some days when I needed some encouragement or even worse, I needed the right words to remain on my journey, I would start to read what I had written on the notecards.

Actually, there was a time in my recent past that I had to pull out those notecards several times a day just to remind myself who I am and that I am God's child. You see, I was in a work situation that would tear me down and make me question who I was on a daily basis. These scriptures and the words of wisdom not only helped me make it through the day but helped me to not lose my mind and helped me not feel the need to change who I am.

A year or so went by and the Lord spoke to me again about these cards that I continued to write. His words to me are that there are a lot of women who are like you and are in need of the same things you are in need of. They doubt themselves, they live in fear instead of living free, they don't have an intimate relationship with Me even though they want it and they lack joy true joy in their lives.

The Lord then told me to start writing letters to these women, my sisters, based on the notecards that I had written. He said they need to hear from another woman who is on a spiritual, emotional and physical journey to be better. They need to know they are not alone. Don't let the devil isolate these women to think they are the only ones who feel this way. Don't let satan influence their thoughts so they go the wrong direction on their journey.

So I decided to follow the leading of the Lord and write this book. I pray that this book helps you personally along your journey. I pray the Lord uses this book to encourage your heart and to focus your mind on the spiritual and not the carnal. And Lord I pray that through this book at least one woman gets a better understanding of who You are and gets a little closer and more intimate with You Lord. Lord God, I thank you for this privilege and I thank You for Your trust in me.

AUTOGRAPH PAGE

Autograph this book to your "sister" as a personal investment into the life of someone that God has put in your path on this life journey.

Table of Contents

YOU ARE FULL OF
YOURSELF AND
NOT FULL OF GOD 3

ASK GOD TO REVEL
THE NEXT STEP 15

LIVE AND LET GO..................31

DO NOT RUN
BACK TO THE
FAMILIAR...............................43

INSPIRE INTIMACY..................53

JOY DEEP IN MY
HEART....................................69

NO MANIPULATION
REQUIRED..............................85

CHRIST IN YOUR
HOME....................................95

INCREASE YOUR SELF-ACCEPTANCE……………………………105

DO NOT ALLOW
THE WAY OTHER
PEOPLE TREAT YOU
DETERMINE YOUR VALUE…………..117

NO FEAR HERE…………………………..127

Thoughts From My Heart

You are Full of Yourself and Not Full of God

August 2009

Dear Sister,

Are there days that you forget about God? I don't mean that you forget there is a God or even that throughout the day, when things go your way or don't go your way you don't thank God or ask God, "Why me?" I mean your day is so consumed with activities, thoughts and plans that you are more consumed with yourself and what you have to do, that you forget to talk to God, pray to God or thank God?

During these days, weeks, months or years, you are more full of yourself than you are full of God. I can tell you, this can frequently happen to me. I become so consumed with work, or what I need to accomplish at home or what I need to do for others that I forget to include God in my thoughts and plans. My problem is I get so concerned about pleasing others and making sure everything is as perfect as I can make it, that I don't have time to sit at the Lords feet and just be still.

There is an awesome book that I have read and reread written by Joanna Weaver titled, *Having a Mary Heart in a Martha World*. This woman has written about my life in this book. The Bible does not talk a lot about Mary and Martha. They are mentioned in *Luke 10:38-42, John 11:1-44 and John 12: 1-11.*

There is a big part of me that wants to be like Mary. Mary was the worshiper. She never seems to have anxiety, worry or actually a care in the world. Mary took her time to smell the roses, be introspective and really enjoy life. She took the time to be quiet and just listen, no matter what there was to do around the house.

Martha, on the other hand, was constantly in motion. There was always something to do and some place to be. She probably had a difficult time delegating to other people because she thought she did it the best. Or maybe it was because if she had someone else do it, she might actually have time to just sit and be quiet. This probably led to a little bit of anxiety because either she did not know how to just sit or she would end up feeling guilty because you know as well as I know, there is always something to do. Boy oh boy, I can relate to Martha. How about you sister?

In the gospel of Luke, he describes the conflict these two women had during a visit from Jesus and His Apostles. Mary was just so taken by the presence of Jesus that she forgot or ignored all that needed to be accomplished around the house to prepare to feed and care for Jesus and the Apostles.

She chose to be quiet and sit at Jesus's feet and absorb all she could from His teaching.

Martha on the other hand was running around like a mad woman, trying to cook, clean, go to the store and get flowers for the table, make sure the napkins were pressed, bring out the good china, polish the silver, clean dirty walls from the dogs and the kids...oops, I forgot who I was talking about for a second. I vividly see my life in this scenario.

Martha went to the Lord to complain about Mary and her lack of support. Pretty much the same way I go to the Lord to complain about my husband and kids when I don't feel they are helping enough. And Jesus said, "Martha, Martha you are worried and upset about many things, but only one thing is needed. Mary has chosen what is better and it will not be taken from her." Martha must have felt like someone punched her in the stomach when the Lord told her that. I know that every time I read that, I feel the wind sucked out of me.

The Lord really does not care if your house is sparking clean, if there are fresh cooked meals every night, if your laundry is piled high or if there are a couple of scuff marks on the floors or the walls. He cares more about your relationship with Him and your willingness to spend time with Him.

Now we all know that things still need to get done and that there needs to be a balance between the Martha and the Mary behaviors. I guess if we were a Nun or a monk or lived in absolute isolation, we could just sit and pray and worship all day every day. The Lord created this world for us to enjoy and to be engaged. While we are enjoying and engaging, we must remain full of God and not full of ourselves.

We must not let the activities that we must do cause us worry and anxiety. When worry and anxiety creep in, there is then no place for God. God can't live in your worrying or anxious brain or heart. When worry and anxiety start to overtake us, we must then take on the Mary behavior and become quiet and focus on the Lord and be willing to listen to His instruction and His wisdom.

But in reality, how do we do that? I mean even though I may in my heart want to spend quiet time with the Lord, I always seem to say well, as soon as I start the laundry and make lunch and do the dishes and feed the dogs and do the ironing, spend time with the kids, love on my husband; then I will spend quite time with God. But it never fails by the time all that is done, and several other things popped up that needed to get accomplished, it is now way past my bedtime and when I do sit down to be quiet with God, I am so exhausted, that my eyes start to get heavy and before you know it I am on the couch fast asleep.

So once again, I think, I failed and this will never work. I will never have the time with God that He and I deserve and so desperately need. By thinking this way though, I am now full of myself again, and not full of God. God is forgiving. God gives us grace and mercy.

So what can we do, all of us Martha women, to be more like Mary? We must put God into everything we do. We must talk to Him all day every day. When we need to make a decision, we must first ask God what He would do. When we are getting anxious about being late for an appointment or a meeting, we must ask God to calm our spirit. When we worry about our husbands when they are late and have not called, we must ask God to keep them safe or stop our minds from thinking bad thoughts. When we get angry with our children we must ask God to give us wisdom on how to correct them. When we are able to do this, we are becoming like Mary even though we may be keeping the Martha pace.

Sister, my prayer for you is that each and every day, your mind, your heart and your spirit becomes more filled up with God that even when you are running around town doing errands, driving the kids to all of their activities and just doing all the things that women do, that you feel like Mary sitting at the feet of Jesus.

Blessings,

Debbie

Thoughts From The Word

THE WISE WOMAN BUILDS HER HOUSE, BUT WITH HER OWN HANDS, THE FOOLISH ONE TEARS HERS DOWN.

PROVERBS 14:1

Sister, Let me confess to you, there have been multiple times that I have done such an extraordinary job in building up my house. My marriage is going great, the kids are behaving and growing nicely and then all of a sudden I allow satan to overtake me, if you know what I mean. Before you know it, all the work I put in to build up my house has been destroyed with a few unkind or misplaced words, actions that are not perceived as compassionate or my own thoughts that cloud how I see a situation and then impact my attitude which then impacts my household.

You know what they say; if mamma is not happy no one is happy. So sister, be a wise woman and realize how quickly all your hard work can be destroyed within seconds.

Think to yourself, is what I am going to say, do or think worth the possibility of destroying all the hard work and progress that I have made? Seek direction from God and His word before you tear your house down.

Thoughts From My Heart

ASK GOD TO REVEAL THE NEXT STEP

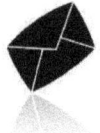

October 2009

Dear Sister,

When you make decisions in your life, do you make these decisions based on what you want, what other people are telling you to do or by what you gut feels? Or are you one of the smart people who pray and ask God for guidance and wisdom? Do you have the faith and the courage to ask God to reveal the next step to you?

Well my sister, I will tell you that I have been one of those people for most of my life that would base major decisions in my life on my gut or advice from others. And honestly, it worked out pretty well from where I stood. Let me make sure you understand what I am saying here. It worked out pretty well for me from WHERE I STOOD not from where I currently stand.

For most of my life, I believed in God and truly feared Him. I guess that guilt and fear I had stemmed mostly from my Catholic upbringing. I always knew that Jesus had died for me but I never really understood the grace and mercy part of it. I just knew that if something went wrong in my life it was because I had done something wrong. And as my mom used to say to me "See, God got you for that".

So when major decisions had to be made in my life, like where I was to go to school , what my career would be, what job I should take, all the way to whom should I marry, I truly depended on myself and myself alone to lead me on my journey. Unfortunately, God did not factor into these decisions.

Please understand, it was not as if I never thought about what God had planned for me. I did have knowledge of God all my life but I really did not know Him and I sure as heck did not depend on Him. I felt that I knew what was best for me. I guess you could say I was a know it all.

You could also say I lived a pretty sheltered life. I really did not have to make any major decisions or plans for my life until it was time to go to college and make plans for my future. My mom was a stay at home mom and she pretty much ruled the roost. Plus she took care of all of our needs. My sister and I pretty much wanted for nothing. So when I was young, I never really had to rely on God or ask God for much. The Lord provided and I did not even realize it.

When it was time to go to college, I must have applied to 5 or 6 different schools all over the country. I did get accepted to most that I applied. I really wanted to go to Pepperdine in California. My gosh, who wouldn't? The dorms were practically on the beach. However, my parents were not willing to pay that tuition or have me that far away from home (we lived in Downers Grove. IL). One of the schools that I applied to was Indiana University in Bloomington Indiana. I had gone to a swim camp there one summer when I was 12 or 13 years old and I fell in love with the campus. So when I got accepted there, it was pretty much a no brainer that that is where I would go.

My original major in college was Sports Medicine and Athletic Training. See, I was a jock most of my life. I swam competitively since I was 5 years old and in high school I played basketball and played badminton. My senior year, I won most valuable player in all three sports as well as I was captain of all three teams. So really all my life I was involved in sports and loved them. I could not see my life any differently than somehow, some way being involved in sports.

During my sophomore year in college you have to see a guidance counselor one more time to plan your last two years and just to make sure you are still on the right track. When I met with the counselor, she asked what my plans were after graduation. I told her I wanted to be a trainer for a college or professional basketball team.

She looked at me as if just told her I wanted to have a sex change and I wanted to make a million dollars a year. She told me that that would never happen. Did I not realize I was a woman? There would never be a chance of me working with a men's team. She then went on to tell me that I could change my major and I could become a nurse. Nurses were desperately needed and I would be guaranteed a job after I graduated. She said there was no way she could guarantee me anything after I graduated with a sports medicine/athletic training degree.

Well, having a job after I graduated was very important to me. My parents told me that I would not be allowed to come home again after graduation and live with them. So I thought long and hard -about two minutes and said ok how do I change my major?

So you understand, I never thought of being a nurse. Yes, as a child I would read the Nurse Nancy book over and over and I did play hospital with my baby dolls and Barbie dolls but still, the thought of actually being a nurse was never in my mind. So how and why did I change my major so fast and not really even think about it? Because I was relying on other people and myself to guide my path. Never during that conversation with the counselor did I ever think, I wonder what God has planned for me. I never asked God to reveal the next step for me.

I went through nursing school and received my BSN from Indiana University. Nursing school was very painful for me. I did well in classes and even did well in clinical, but inside, I was a nervous wreck when I had to take care of patients, give them shots and tell them bad news.

Deep down, I knew that bedside nursing was not my calling. I regretted my decision to become a nurse but I was too far in to it to make a change. Even though I never asked God for guidance, I look back now and realize how He protected me and how He really had a hand in my life.

When I got out of nursing school, I moved to Florida and stated working at a hospital in Tampa. It was a matter of months before I was in a leadership position on the nursing units. I still had to care for patients, but I had other responsibilities as well which kept me interested and growing as a nurse and a leader. It was at this hospital that I found out about rehab nursing and the similarities rehab nursing had to sports medicine and coaching. I took care of spinal cord injury patients, brain injury and stroke patients. A lot of the care that we provided for these patients had to do with coaching them and motivating them to get back to their previous level of function.

Once again, when I went into rehab nursing, I never prayed or asked the Lord if this is the direction I should go. I just jumped into it and hoped for the best. But even though I was denying the Lord, the Lord did not deny me. This may not have been the path He had planned for me, but He was not going to let me fail or be miserable. He was still protecting me and guiding me even though I was not asking for it.

Over the years, many other career decisions were made as well as the decisions to go back to school to get my master's degree, the decision to get married and the decision to get divorced. As I was dating my current husband, I was beginning to understand the Lord better and even though I did not want to admit it, I realized I did not have a very good relationship with the Lord. I realized my faith and trust in Him was lacking and since I did not really talk and pray to Him often, I did not realize what He had done for me or what He wanted to do for me.

During the time my current husband and I were dating, there was a large piece of me that wanted to get married. However, he was not as anxious to get married as I was and there was a time that our relationship got strained because of my persistent asking. Being the stubborn, pig headed person that I am, I thought ok God, I am going to put this one into your hands.

I had been going to church with my then boyfriend and now husband and I was hearing a lot about trusting God, God is in control, God does things in His timing not yours. So we were going away for a weekend together to Naples. Prior to our trip and even during our trip, I just kept praying to God and telling Him, Lord this relationship is in Your hands. If this man is the right man for me, make it clear to him and make it clear to me. I told the Lord, I am tired of trying to run this relationship and I am giving the relationship and this man over to You. Our trip to Naples was phenomenal. And the next couple of weeks were even better. After I put this relationship in the Lord's hands, this man proposed to me three weeks later.

Well, well well, I finally realized what I had been missing for so many years. After I gave the relationship over to the Lord, I had no worries or concerns. I truly left it up to God. And God came through. I do believe that if God had said, this is not the man for you, I would have put up a little bit of a fight, but I sincerely gave this to the Lord and I was determined to finally ask Him and listen to what He had to tell me. God really does care and He wants you to cast all your concerns onto Him. Ain't God good?

Since then, there have been times when I once again relied more on myself than on God to make decision. But as my faith grows and my relationship with the Lord gets more intimate, I rely on Him to reveal every next step I am to take. I am currently in a job situation where I am just tolerated and not celebrated.

Many times I have prayed and asked God to reveal to me what my next step is. He has told me, that my next step right now is to stay where I am. He will protect me from any evil or ill will but my purpose right now is to bring home a pay check and support my husband in his ministry endeavors. The Lord keeps reveling to me little by little, that I won't be in this position for very long and that when the time is right, He will reveal my next step but right now those stepping stones are too far away for me to jump onto.

If I was not relying on God, I would have left this job and gone somewhere else. And you know what, I would not be any happier because the Lord would not have been involved with my decision. I can live each day in peace and joy, knowing the Lord has my back. He always has and He always will.

Sisters, these scriptures below give you insight into trusting the Lord and allowing Him to lead you on your path. Study them and let them permeate your spirit.

Blessings,

Debbie

Unless the Lord builds the house, those who build it labor in vain. Unless the Lord guards the city, the guard keeps watch in vain. It is in vain that you rise up early and go late to rest, eating the bread of anxious toil; for he gives sleep to his beloved. (Psalm 127:1-2)

Trust in the Lord with all your heart and lean not on your own understanding; in all your ways acknowledge him, and he will make your paths straight. (Proverbs 3:5-6)

Your father knows what you need before you ask him. So do not worry, saying 'What shall we eat?' or 'What shall we wear?' For the pagans run after all these things, and your heavenly Father knows that you need them. But seek first his kingdom and his righteousness, and all these things will be given to you as well. Therefore do not worry about tomorrow, for tomorrow will worry about itself. Today's trouble is enough for today. (Matthew 6:8b, 31-34)

Wait for the Lord; be strong, and let your heart take courage; wait for the Lord!
(Psalm 27:14)

Abide in me as I abide in you. Just as the branch cannot bear fruit by itself unless it abides in the vine, neither can you unless you abide in me. I am the vine, you are the branches. Those who abide in me and I in them bear much fruit, because apart from me you can do nothing. If you abide in me, and my words abide in you, ask for whatever you wish, and it will be done for you. If you keep my commandments, you will abide in my love, just as I have kept my Father's commandments and abide in his love.
(John 15:4-5,7,10)

Be still, and know that I am God.
(Psalm 46:10)

You who live in the shelter of the Most High, who abide in the shadow of the Almighty, will say to the Lord, "My refuge and my fortress; my God in whom I trust." You will not fear the terror of the night, or the arrow that flies by day, or the pestilence that stalks in darkness, or the destruction that wastes at noonday. Because you have made the Lord your refuge, the Most High your dwelling place, no evil shall befall you, no scourge come near your tent. For he will command his angels concerning you to guard you in all your ways. On their hands they will bear you up, so that you will not dash your foot against a stone.
(Psalm 91:1-2,5-6,9-12)

Thoughts From The Word

A GENTLE ANSWER TURNS AWAY WRATH, BUT A HARSH WORD STIRS UP ANGER

PROVERBS 15:1

1,2,3,4,5,6,7,8,9,10

Ok, Sister, did you count to ten with me? I know the hair is standing up on the back of your neck, your pulse is racing and your eyes are ready to pop out of your head, but let the anger go. Don't allow your anger to come out in a harsh, sarcastic, mean and hurtful tone. Anger is an emotion that we have to control.

Don't let your anger ruin your relationships that you have been working hard to improve. Use words that are kind and gentle but still truthful. By being gentle but true you will preserve your relationship and allow God to step in and do His miraculous healing as well as allowing God to make the appropriate changes.

Thoughts From My Heart

Letters to My Sister

LIVE AND LET GO

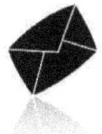

January 2010

Dear Sister,

Is your past haunting you? Is it causing you to want to curl up into a ball and hide in a corner? Or is your past causing you to feel unworthy of love and of anyone caring for you? Or in your past, have you been hurt so bad that you can't let the anger and hurt go? Well my sister, I am writing to tell you that you can't change the past but bitterness is changing you. LIVE AND LET GO.

I have pretty much spent my life looking back and living in the past hurts and disappointments of my life. I was made fun of as a child because I was overweight. Well actually I was fat. Of course all the adults would try to make me feel better by saying you are not fat, you are just big boned. But it did not matter what the adults were telling me, other 8, 9 and 10 year olds just called me fat.

Until recently I still saw myself as the "fat" kid that all my friends made fun of. Even though now all the "fat" as shifted to the right places, I still find it hard to call myself beautiful. And my weight is something I continue to struggle with to this day. I look at a milkshake and it goes to my thighs and I start to jiggle all over.

I need to break this habit of looking back to when I was young and fat. I can't change that I was overweight and I can't change all the mean comments that people would say about me. I used to be angry about it and I can still feel the sting of those comments like they were just said yesterday. However, since having a more intimate relationship with Jesus, He has helped me Live and Let Go.

Those kids were mean to me by making fun of me, but at 43 years old it was time to forgive them and not let their words still infiltrate my though process and the way I thought of myself. The anger and bitterness was holding me back from achieving what the Lord had in store for me.

And I found myself being a hypocrite because since my daughter was a little girl I have been preaching to her that it does not matter what you look like on the outside, it is the inside that the Lord cares about. Your looks can be taken away from you at any time, but if you have a kind and caring heart, that can never change.

The Lord brought this to my attention. How can I be preaching this to my daughter and expect her to believe it, if I do not believe it and I am not living it? My concentration had been on my external for so long and unfortunately that is what people noticed about me first. I knew I needed to change this for me and for my daughter. Well, I am still big boned and yes, I still work

hard at trying to keep my weight in check, but it is not the focus of my life. The Lord is the focus and what the Lords purpose for me is my focus. I am on the Lords journey and He is directing my path.
But being made fun of about my weight is hardly the only thing that I look back on that causes me bitterness, anger and resentment. My mom died at age 48 with breast cancer. She was diagnosed on my birthday when I was turning 29 and she died the following year 6 days after my 30th birthday. I was 5 ½ months pregnant with my first child and her first grandchild.

My mom felt a lump in her breast months and maybe even a year before she was dragged to the doctor by my father. See my mom was stubborn, hard headed, pig headed you name it, to the core. And no one was going to tell her what to do. She even said once that she would rather not know what was wrong with her and not go through treatment. She would rather just die. So as you can see, my mom was a little selfish too.

Up until a couple of years ago, I was very resentful of my mom as well as my dad. I was angry with my dad for not being a stronger person, a stronger man and make my mom go to the doctor when the lump was first discovered. In my mind, if he would have done that then my mom would still be alive today.

You see, my mom was my best friend and I did not handle losing my best friend very well. Plus I wanted her to be around to meet her granddaughter, someone who would be both of our new best friend. But that did not happen. My mom went thought chemo and radiation.

However, the cancer metastasized to her brain. She had brain surgery which left her unable to talk which was awful because if there was one thing my mom could do was talk. The last couple of months of her life, I missed hearing her voice.

When she died, bitterness over took me. Stress over took me as well. I ended up having my daughter 7 weeks premature. During the first couple of months after my daughter's birth, I needed my mom more than ever, but she was gone. So I lived in fear, anger, hurt, resentment and bitterness.

As the years went by, the fear of not making right decisions dissipated, the hurt stared to fade, but I lived with resentment toward my mom and dad and bitterness kept rearing its ugly head. I ended up getting divorced and eventually getting remarried. With the help of my new husband and the Lord, I stared to work thought the feelings of bitterness.

Today, I still miss my mom and wish she could see what a fantastic granddaughter she has. More so, I wish my daughter could have the privilege of knowing my mom, her grandma. They are so much alike and I know they would have been best of friends. But through all of this the Lord has shown me why He is God and how He knows what is best for us. This is really hard to say, but if my mom was still alive, I would not know Jesus and rely on Him the way I do today. My daughter would be more spoiled and pampered than she needs to be. I may not have gotten a divorce hence I would not have met the man who has done so much for my life, who has shown me what it really means to live a Christian life and how to truly trust the Lord and be patient and let Him guide and direct your path.

I can't change that my mom died or that my dad was not more forceful with her. The past is the past. I have to change how I think about my past and not let bad situations and bad choices haut me forever.

Dear sister, I know that you may not be very proud of your past or that you have allowed circumstances in your life affect your outlook and attitude about this life that God has given you. But today, you can make the change. You need to tell yourself, I can't change the past. Bitterness is changing me. I need to live and let go.

As in 1 Peter 4:3-5 **For you have spent enough time in the past doing what pagans choose to do- living in debauchery, lust, drunkenness, orgies, carousing and detestable idolatry. They think it is strange that you do not plunge with them into the same flood of dissipation and they heap abuse on you. But they have to give account to him who is ready to judge the living and the dead.**

It is time sister to live in the present and leave your past behind. Forgive others and most importantly forgive yourself. The Lord has. Live and Let Go.

Blessings,

Debbie

Thoughts From The Word

GOD IS OUR REFUGE AND OUR STRENGTH AND EVER PRESENT HELP IN TROUBLE

PSALM 46:1

Sister,

Whether you have been hurt, feel all alone, feel like no one understands you or just tired and frustrated, seek Gods face and take refuge in His love for you no matter what you have done or what you are going through. He will be your protector, your refuge and when you don't have the strength to go on or make another move, God WILL be your strength.

Thoughts From My Heart

Letters to My Sister

DO NOT RUN BACK TO THE FAMILIAR

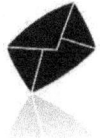

March 2010

Dear Sister,

As I sit here at this computer typing this letter to you encourage your spirit, I just realized I am guilty of doing what I am encouraging you NOT to do. I am writing to you today to tell you DO NOT RUN BACK TO THE FAMILIAR. The familiar may be negative thinking, the familiar may be a bad attitude, the familiar may be sarcasm, the familiar may be fear, the familiar may be hurt and depression, the familiar may be loneliness, the familiar may be drugs and alcohol, and the familiar may be finding comfort in premarital sex or adulterous sex. I could go on and on.

We do well for a while. We think we have our weaknesses licked. We start to feel good. We are patting ourselves on the back when we face a situation and we don't have a familiar response but a response that we and the Lord have been working on. We get confident and almost cocky about how good we are doing.

We Praise God and thank Him for keeping our mind and keeping us on track. We do really well for a while, sometime a long while but what we have to remember is that the devil sees your success and boy is he getting angrier about it with each passing day. So he may just keep trying to throw curve balls at you to see if you will start that slow jog back to the familiar things that comfort you. Unless you are firmly planted in the Lord and you are praying every day throughout the day, you are reading His word and you spend some quite time with Him the devil can and will start the infiltration.

Your excuse is probably similar to mine. Full time job, full time home life, try to fit in work outs, church responsibilities, children activities, community organization meetings...can I go on. What I have realized is that when life becomes overwhelming I run to the Lord with my arms wide open and desperate for His love and His help and His peace. He has never failed me.

The question is why do I allow myself to get there? Probably because it is familiar to me. My life was chaotic before I really knew the Lord. I thrived in negative thinking and chaos (so I thought). I lived this way for over 30 something years so it really was my familiar. However, knowing the Lord and the peace and joy that He can provide, I really want this to be my new familiar.

So sister, how do we not run back to the familiar? What has become obvious for me is that the devil has his way with me when I allow life to consume me. When I allow myself to be over scheduled and overburdened as well as when I allow myself to be consumed with too many fleshly things.

It does seem like I spend a lot of time in my car or waiting for an appointment or for a meeting to start.

I love to read and I love to read magazines. We have been getting a lot of magazines at our home lately and I find myself reading these magazines all the time whereas before, I would have a book or the bible or an article from a Christian writer that I would be reading during those couple minutes of down time. I have allowed myself to be distracted and not focused on the Lord and the Word.

Now sister, you know I believe in balance and I believe you have to have your way to relax and let your hair down so please hear me. I am just saying that I know I felt I was doing so well and the Lord was blessing me and I was still praising Him and thanking Him for all He was doing in my life BUT I was not reading His word or doing some of those things I know had brought me closer to Him.
So what happened? Sickness, feelings of loneliness crept in, feeling a lack of affection and attention, chaos striking at work and then being over committed. What was easier for me to do? Run, I mean really sprint back to that negative thinking, feeling angry and lonely and letting my thoughts, not the Lords thoughts control my mood and my words and my actions.

So sister, I encourage you to stay focused on the Lord through praying and spending quiet time with Him. Please, please read His word. You do not have to spend hours, just a couple minutes. Just keep the word in your spirit and on your tongue. If you do the devil will not be able to penetrate your thoughts or your words and your new familiar will be much better than your old.

Blessings,

Debbie

Thoughts From The Word

THE TONGUE OF THE WISE COMMANDS KNOWLEDGE, BUT THE MOUTH OF THE FOOL GUSHES FOLLY

PROVERBS 15:2

Sister,

I don't know about you but my mouth sure gets me into a lot of TROUBLE. Sister, please just use your common sense and if you don't know what you are talking about, BE QUIET.

Don't use your mouth to spread gossip. Don't use your mouth to speak badly of someone. Don't use your mouth to spew out negativity. Don't use your mouth to speak nonsense. And please don't use your mouth just because you like to hear yourself talk but you say nothing. Be wise my sister and speak what you know and let others be seen as fools.

Letters to My Sister

Letters to My Sister

Thoughts From My Heart

INSPIRE INTIMACY

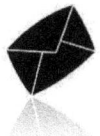

May 2010

Dear Sister,

When you talk about being intimate with someone the word intimacy usually conjures up sex. Some of you may think an intimate relationship can be achieved with a one night stand. However, real true intimacy must be achieved over time. Some of you may think of a marriage relationship when intimacy is brought up. Intimacy in this context has to do with spiritual, physical, mental and emotional intimacy. You don't meet someone off the street and all of a sudden have an intimate relationship. You may have a sexual encounter but trust me there is no intimacy that is created.

As women, we desire intimacy in a relationship more than anything. Marital intimacy is accomplished as a husband and wife seek to sacrificially love each other by learning to meet each other's needs within the marriage. Intimacy really means total life sharing.

Marital intimacy is achieved in all of its completeness as each spouse learns to share and connect with each other in the four areas of emotional, spiritual, mental and physical intimacy. Women generally seek fulfillment of emotional connection and want to know that feelings are both valued and shared in an intimate relationship. They also enjoy communicating closeness through mental forms of intimacy and feel connected through mutual exchange of thoughts. This allows them to enter into the daily world where their husbands live and think.

Men are wired somewhat differently and tend to experience the greatest levels of intimacy through companionship, activity and forms of physical intimacy, such as sexual intercourse. While the intimacy needs of women might be described as being, the same needs in men can best be conceptualized as doing.

God wants to have an intimate relationship with you as well. God sees you as a precious treasure and he longs to have a close relationship with you. More than anything He wants you to have an intimate love relationship and friendship with Him. God wants you to spend time with Him and intimately communicate with Him to enjoy fellowship with Him, to trust Him and follow Him.

To have intimacy in your marriage, you must first understand love and more importantly Gods love. You can not give this type of love if you have never experienced being loved that way. God's love is "other person" focused. It is giving rather than self-seeking. God, who knows you, who knows everything about you, loves you perfectly. God tells us through the ancient prophet Jeremiah, **"*I have loved you with an everlasting love; and I draw you unto myself*"** (Jeremiah 31:3). So Gods love for you is never going to change. God continues to love us no matter what. As you can see, God's view of love is totally different from what society tells us love is. Can you imagine a relationship with this type of love? God simply tells us that His forgiveness and love is ours for the asking. It is His gift to us. But if we refuse the gift, we are the ones who cut ourselves off from finding true fulfillment, true intimacy and true purpose in life.

After we place our faith and love in Him, He takes up residence within our lives and we have intimacy with Him. His forgiveness is there to cleanse us from our deepest sins, the deepest self- centeredness and the deepest problem or struggle we ever had or will have.

When we entrust ourselves to Jesus Christ, He gives us new love and new power day by day. This is where the intimacy we are looking for is satisfied. God gives us love that will not quit, and will not stop with the growing years and the changing times.

His love can bring two people together, with Him at the center of the union. With Him as its center, your life will take on a whole new dimension – a spiritual one, bringing more harmony and fulfillment to all of your relationships.

I don't know about you sister, but I just expect intimacy to happen, whether it be in my marriage or in my relationship with God. To me it is an expectation and not something I am very willing to wait on. I am typically a patient person, but when it comes to making my relationships more intimate, I really feel it should be automatic. If I show love and respect most of the time and I communicate pretty well and I remain physically attractive then my reward should be intimacy, right? With this, I am reminded of a quote I read somewhere, "It is better to inspire intimacy than require intimacy in a relationship."

Let's quickly breakdown what inspire means: to encourage, to motivate, to make you want to do better. So often in my marriage as well with my relationship with God, I require intimacy. I require a certain amount of communication with my spouse, I require a certain amount of touching from my spouse, and I require a certain amount of time spent with my spouse.

If these things occur, then I should have intimacy. The same thing goes for God. I often wonder why I sometimes I don't "hear" from God. Why I don't have clear direction in my life. I pray daily and multiple times during the day. I do my very best to read His word. I worship Him regularly so that should mean I have intimacy with God.

I do tend to ask a lot from the Lord; Lord Fix this person, change this situation, Lord can you tell me what I should be doing next. But I am communicating with Him regularly, am I not? Sister, I tell you, none of this in my marriage or in my relationship with God has inspired any intimacy.

Let's talk a little first about how to inspire intimacy with God. I can inspire intimacy with God by having faith. All true intimacy with God has its basis in faith. In fact no relationship with Him is possible apart from faith. **We love Him by faith, even though we have not seen Him** (1 Peter: 1:8). Scripture teaches us that our sins were imputed to Jesus, and He paid the full penalty for them in His death. Now Jesus' own righteousness is imputed to us and we receive full merit of it. Without this reality, we could not enjoy a relationship with a holy God. I can inspire intimacy with God by having faith in all that I do.

I can inspire intimacy with God through true worship. To truly worship our Lord, I must know the Scriptures. Those of us who want to know the Lord in the true way must be thoroughly familiar with His Word. If we want God to delight in our worship, we must think rightly about Him. Our worship should not consist of rote acts of religious ritual but real worship is grounded in the true knowledge of God. To be intimate with God, we can worship Him because we really know Him.

I can inspire intimacy with God through prayer. Jesus himself taught us to seek intimacy with God through private prayer. Prayer is where the worshipper pours out her heart to God. And Jesus Himself stressed the importance of private prayer: *"when thou prayest, enter into thy closet, and when thou hast shut thy door, pray to thy Father which is in secret"* (Matthew 6:6). The true Christian who inspires intimacy with God will pray most often and most fervently in private. And if we understood what an incomprehensible privilege it is to be invited to come boldly before His throne of grace, we would surly spend more time there pouring out our most intimate thoughts, fears, desires and expressions of love to Him.

I can inspire intimacy with God through obedience. Jesus said to His disciples, ***"Ye are my friends, if ye do whatsoever I command you"*** (John 15:14). Thus Jesus Himself made obedience to Him an absolute requirement for true spiritual intimacy. No one can claim intimacy with God whose life is marked by disobedience rather than submission to Him. True intimacy with Him is utterly impossible without unconditional surrender to His divine authority.

I can inspire intimacy with God through suffering. ***"That I may know him, and the power of His resurrection, and the fellowship of His sufferings, being made conformable unto His death"*** (Philippians 3:10). This scripture explains to us that God's grace is sufficient to see us through all our sufferings. Moreover, God's strength is made perfect in our weakness. There is a special blessing known only to those who suffer for Christ's sake. Those who would desire true intimacy with Him must be willing to endure what He endured.

So know what about our marriages? How can we inspire intimacy there? True marital intimacy only can occur when a husband and wife surrender their lives and their relationship to God. Your marriage relationship becomes intimate when you grow together spiritually and your goal is to please God and not each other.

Personally for me, that can still be hard to conceptualize. I am a people pleaser. I will do just about anything to make someone else happy, even to my detriment. So taking the focus off of the person and what would make them happy and put the focus on God and what would make Him happy can at times leave me confused. But I am getting there. What I realized is sometimes what would make my husband happy is not what God wants for him. I have to love my husband enough to give him what God wants for him and not what I want for him.

Before we can have intimacy in our marriage, we first must have an intimate relationship with God. Sister that is why the first part of this letter is about you and God. It is important that both husband and wife are growing spiritually as individuals. That is the first step of intimacy. The second step happens when you experience God together and you share with each other what you learned about Him. The spiritual connection is what keeps your marriage together.

It allows you to connect at the deepest level, it connects you with what God's purpose and plan for your life is as a couple, it allows you to bless each other with God's love, and it brings your values and desires into agreement through deep levels of communication.

So now the real difficult part, making time to connect spiritually. Sister, I know you have a busy life and this is just one more thing to add to your "TO DO LIST" but in reality, this is the most important thing you need to make time for. If you are not taking time to grow spiritually individually and then not taking the time to connect spiritually with your spouse or significant other, all other aspects of your life are likely to suffer.

Please take my advice because been there done that and have multiple t-shits that show my failures. I have the tendency to start off strong, you know have it all scheduled out in my calendar, 6 am get up and read bible, 10 am pray for 15 min, 3 pm pray for 15 min, 5 pm pray and meditate before heading home from work, and 930 pm pray and do devotion with my husband.

Looks great on paper, right? Now the question becomes how do I do this when life gets in the way? When you have back to back meetings at work and don't even have 5 min to pee let alone have quiet time to pray. When 6 am comes around and you are too tired to get out of bed because you did not go to bed till 2 am because you were trying to get multiple things accomplished. Or when 930 pm comes around and your husband still have things that need to be done, the kids are still up doing homework and you don't see things quieting down till after 11 and you really need to get some sleep. So now what?

Don't give up. Just because your schedule did not work out for a couple of days or a couple of weeks, do your best to get back on track or reevaluate your plan. I like a schedule, it helps me get everything accomplished but sometimes I have to reevaluate my plan and make some changes. For example, I know there is no way my husband and I can do devotion each night. We both have too much going on but we can do it once a week and we do pray every night as a family.

But just to warn you, do not fall off your praying and devotion for very long. Trust me on this one. Once you start having an intimate relationship with God and all of a sudden you don't have time for Him, He is a jealous

God and I have seen firsthand how He can let chaos and problems happen that would have not occurred if I had spent time with Him.

"You shall not make for yourself an idol, or any likeness of what is in heaven above or on the earth beneath or in the water under the earth. You shall not worship them or serve them; for I, the LORD your God, am a jealous God" (Exodus 20:4-5).

Intimacy will come in a marriage when you pray together, read the bible together and talk about what God is teaching you. As well you can do a bible study or devotional together and be accountable to each other for your personal spiritual growth.

Sister, you can inspire intimacy in your relationship by having intimacy with God. If you have this type of intimacy you will no longer require intimacy from your spouse, but your spouse will give you the intimacy you desire because of YOUR relationship with God. Intimacy is important to women but it is more important to God.

Blessings,

Debbie

Letters to My Sister

Thoughts From The Word

CREATE IN ME A PURE HEART, OH GOD AND RENEW A STEADFAST SPIRIT WITHIN ME

PSALM 51:10

Sister,

No matter what you have done and no matter what life has done to you, have faith in the Lord our God and He will renew your life, your mind, your speech, your body, your health, your soul, your relationships, and your family. Be steadfast. Never ever give up because God never gives up on you.

Thoughts From My Heart

Joy Deep in My Heart

August 2011

Dear Sisters,

Did you ever hear the children's bible song,
I've got the joy, joy, joy, joy down in my heart
Where?
Down in my heart!
Where?
Down in my heart!
I've got the joy, joy, joy, joy down in my heart
Down in my heart to stay

Believe it or not, I never heard this song growing up. Maybe it is because I was raised Catholic and really did not go to Sunday school. Or maybe because instead of listening to Christian music my mom would have Michael Jackson, Rod Stewart or Barry Manilow penetrating the walls of our house.

Maybe, just maybe, if I would have heard this song, I would have understood the difference between joy and happiness growing up. Maybe if I understood this when I was young, I would not be struggling with the joy factor now.

Letters to My Sister

I did not really understand the difference between joy and happiness until a few years ago. You may all know this but this is just in case a few of my sisters are as clueless as me about joy and happiness. I will explain. Happiness is fleeting. You feel happy based on the circumstances around you or what is happening to you. With joy (down in your heart) you could be in a very unhappy situation or feeling down and out, but if you have joy, it does not leave you. With joy, you are still able to see the good in a bad situation. With joy deep inside you, your light continues to shine.

I write to you today to encourage you to not let the joy be stolen from your life. You may wake up and not feel happy everyday but you can wake up and feel joyful, joyful knowing that tomorrow you may wake up happy. Evangelist, Minister, preacher, writer, Joyce Meyers wrote a book called <u>The 7 Factors that Steal our Joy</u>. It is an excellent book and I highly encourage you to read it. In the book, she talks about several things that steal your joy. Several of her seven joy stealers I allow to affect my life on a daily basis hence leaving me without joy deep in my heart.

One of the joy stealers is allowing yourself to complicate simple issues. If I had a quarter for every time I did this over my life time, I would be a multi-millionaire. It seems I always try to overachieve and overdo.

Whether it be holding a dinner party for 6 people and having to make at least 3 different entrees and at least 4 dessert, (because what if they don't like pork or what if they don't like pound cake or what if they really like chocolate for dessert), to trying to find something to wear and knowing that I should wear black pumps but because I have three different types of black pumps, I stress out over which is going to look the absolute best.

When you complicate situations, you then let worry creep in, doubt creep in and you create undo stress for yourself. Putting on dinner parties and entertaining people makes me very happy. So as I worry about the food and the atmosphere, I am happy creating and doing, but deep down in my heart my joy is being diminished. After the party and all have gone and all I have left is the cleanup, my happiness diminishes. Because I have been so stressed and worried about the parties' success, I don't have the joy to pick me up and carry me to my next event or situation that may cause me to experience happiness again.

So what can I do and what can you do to not allow complicating simple issues steal your joy? There is another book that I have read called _Having a Mary Heart in a Martha World_ written by Joann Weaver. I relate so much to Martha because she was always doing something and always making issues seem bigger than they were. Jesus loved both Martha and Mary but He definitely had to correct Martha more.

When Jesus came to their house, Martha was busily scurrying around the house, making sure everything was perfect. My goodness, it needed to be more than perfect, this was the Son of God that was visiting their house but Jesus was not concerned with how clean their house was or how good their food was. He just wanted them to all sit and talk and listen and learn.

Mary did just that. She sat at Jesus' feet and listened to Him and absorbed all He had to say, while Martha was too busy and too stressed to enjoy the atmosphere and the teaching.

Then Martha got pretty angry with Mary. Martha felt she was doing all the work and Mary just got to sit. So Martha approached Jesus probably because she wanted Him to see all she was doing for Him and the Apostles. She was looking for a compliment and she was looking for Jesus to chastise Mary. But quite the opposite occurred. Jesus gently rebukes Martha saying to her that Mary has chosen "what is better".

Don't complicate the simple issues in your life. As the saying goes, Keep it simple stupid (KISS). Let the joy of the Lord penetrate you to the core. If joy is deep in your heart, no worry, doubt or stress will eliminate your joy.

You will show me the path of life; in Your presence is fullness of joy, at Your right hand there are pleasures forevermore. (Psalm 16: 11.)

[The Lord God says] And the redeemed of the Lord shall return and come with singing to Zion; everlasting joy shall be upon their heads. They shall obtain joy and gladness, and sorrow and sighing shall flee away. (Isaiah 51: 11)

Some other things that can steal your joy are your tendency not to forgive quickly. Harboring unforgiveness can truly throw you into a deep depression. The Holy Spirit, who creates that joy deep in your heart can not dwell where there is unforgiveness.

I don't know about you but I sure can hold grudges. I actually am very quick to forgive people who are just my acquaintance. It is those family members or dear friends that I have had a hard time really forgiving 100%. I know that is why there are times my joy light flickers out.

I remember for the longest time I could not forgive a friend of mine who in the 8th grade made fun of my saddle shoes. I was always a little ahead of the fashion trends due to my mom. She was a seamstress and she was always a season or so ahead based on fashion week in New York. So my BFF went behind my back and made fun of my black and white saddle shoes. Well, thankfully we went to different high schools and I hardly ever had to see her. But when I did see her out in the neighborhood, I ignored her. I could not forgive.

Well, God has a way of really bringing your unforgiveness to the forefront. I was attending a special event about 10 years later back in my home town and needed my long hair put in an up do. So I went to the local salon and requested to have someone do my hair.

Well who was working at that salon and was an expert at putting up hair? My ex –BFF who made fun of me. Talk about an uncomfortable situation. We talked a little while she was doing my hair but never mentioned our past friendship. Nor did I take this opportunity to let her know I forgave her. Because the sad truth was, I had not forgiven her.

I could still feel the pain of her comments to me from over ten years ago. I left the salon that day, feeling terrible. There was definitely no joy in my heart at that time. Being a very stubborn, hard headed person, it was probably another 10 years till I actually forgave her for her comments to me. In order to truly experience joy, I really need to forgive much quicker. God is quite clear in His Word about forgiveness.

He who covers and forgives an offense seeks love, but he who repeats or harps on a matter separates even close friends. (Proverbs 17: 9)

For if you forgive people their trespasses [their reckless and willful sins, leaving them, letting them go, and giving up resentment], your heavenly Father will also forgive you. (Matthew 6: 14)

Then Peter came up to Him and said, Lord, how many times may my brother sin against me and I forgive him and let it go? [As many as] up to seven times? Jesus answered him, I tell you, not up to seven times, but seventy times seven! (Matthew 18: 21-22)

So also My heavenly Father will deal with every one of you if you do not freely forgive your brother from your heart his offenses. Matthew 18: 35Be gentle and forbearing with one another and, if one has a difference (a grievance or complaint) against another, readily pardoning each other; even as the Lord has [freely] forgiven you, so must you also [forgive]. (Colossians 3: 13)

And whenever you stand praying, if you have anything against anyone, forgive him and let it drop (leave it, let it go), in order that your Father Who is in heaven may also forgive you your [own] failings and shortcomings and let them drop. (Mark 11:25)

Jealousy and envy can also steal your joy. Wanting what someone else has is not being content with what God has given you. Jealousy and envy show God ungratefulness towards how He has made you and towards what He has given you and allowed you to become.

Being an overweight kid, I was frequently jealous of the girls who were thin and very envious of the kids who could eat what ever they wanted and never gain a pound. Also being a very competitive kid (and adult) I would often get mad and jealous when someone did better than me in a race, had a faster time than me or played a better game than me. It was important that I be the shining star. If that limelight got transferred over to someone else and was not shining on me, my joy would go away.

We all get a little envious sometimes when someone gets a blessing that you feel should be yours. That is just part of being human. However, how long you let that jealous or envious sprit fester within you determines your ability to be glad, happy for this person and their blessing. God wants to see how you handle other peoples success before He gives you your own. God made you perfect in His eyes. He wants to see how much you appreciate His gift before He gives you another one.

Jealousy is pretty common among women. Women can get jealous of other women based on the clothes they wear, the shoes they wear, what their hair looks like, the color of their hair, how well behaved their children are, how handsome and attentive their husbands are, the type of vacations someone goes on....I could go on an on and on. But don't let these thoughts and feelings steal your joy. God wants us to be content.

When we are content, the Holy Spirit can provide us peace in our spirit and allow us to hear from God so that He can bless us mightily. The story of Joseph is all about jealousy. Joseph's father Jacob made him a special coat of many colors and Josephs 11 brothers became very jealous of Joseph and ended throwing him in a well. I think most of you know this story (if not go to your bible and read Genesis chapter 37-45) and at the end, Joseph was the one who was blessed by the Lord because he forgave his brothers.

But if you have bitter jealousy and selfish ambition in your hearts, do not boast and be false to the truth. This is not the wisdom that comes down from above, but is earthly, unspiritual, demonic. For where jealousy and selfish ambition exist, there will be disorder and every vile practice. (James 3:14-16)

My sisters, do you have joy deep in your heart? Is it so\ deeply embedded that nothing can steal it, not even evil ways and evil thoughts that are part of us just because we are human?

Meditate on these bible verses and I pray joy is written all over your face for all to see.

May the God of your hope so fill you with all joy and peace in believing [through the experience of your faith] that by the power of the Holy Spirit you may abound and be overflowing (bubbling over) with hope. (Romans 15: 13)

I have told you these things, that My joy and delight may be in you, and that your joy and gladness may be of full measure and complete and overflowing. (John 15: 11)

For this day is holy to our Lord. And be not grieved and depressed, for the joy of the Lord is your strength and stronghold. (Nehemiah 8: 10)

Blessings,

Debbie

Thoughts From The Word

OUR GOD IS OUR REFUGE AND OUR STRENGTH AND EVER PRESENT HELP IN TROUBLE.

PSALM 46:1

Run to HIM sister. He will never fail you. No matter what the trouble is no matter the situation or circumstance, HE is your strength and your covering.

.

Letters to My Sister

Thoughts From My Heart

Letters to My Sister

NO MANIPULATION REQUIRED

December 2010

Dear Sisters,

Don't you wish you could live right all the time? I mean in order to write these letters, I have written down on index cards in a small binder a lot of key quotes and bible verses that mean something special and important to me. Then I have taken these sayings and wrote to you some of the thoughts and hopefully shared some wisdom. However, I want you to be aware, I struggle with some of the messages and I barely do the right thing all of the time.

For example, let me take the next thought that was written in my index card notebook. The thought is, focus more on his needs than manipulate him into meeting mine. I am not exactly sure where I read this statement. Probably in one of those self-help marriage books that I have read. I whole heartedly agree with this statement, and I will tell you, I whole heartedly fail at this more than I succeed.

I guess to really understand this statement we have to understand the definition of manipulation. I could give you the Webster's version, but I think my definition gives more meaning to this statement. *To Manipulate*: To get someone, especially a man, to do what you want and need him to do for you, regardless of his feelings or what he may need or want. Owe, Ouch that hurts to even write.

There have been times when I purposely used manipulation to get what I want and there are times I use manipulation and don't really even realize it. There seems to be a spirit of manipulation that comes upon me and I don't even realize it, until I am well into it. I have heard it called the spirit of Jezebel. If you have never read the story of Jezebel, you may want to get your bible Sister and open up to 1 Kings 21: 1-26 and 2 Kings 9: 7-37.

Basically, Jezebel not only manipulated her husband but she also manipulated elders and nobles to get what she wanted. I think you can look at this story two ways. In one aspect Jezebel was trying to help her husband out because she knew he really wanted the vineyard near their house but the owner of the vineyard would not give it to him. She saw her husband sad and depressed, so she wanted to meet her husband's needs, so she had the owner of the vineyard killed so he could get what he desperately wanted.

Another way to look at this is she manipulated her husband and was leading her husband down a path that the Lord did not want him to go. She may have thought, I will do this for my husband and just imagine now what he will do for me. Well, none of this worked out well for her because if you do not know the story, in the end she is thrown from a building and the dogs eat her.

And by the way, it was not her husband who got her killed, it was the Lord who saw what she had done and He did not approve of her manipulative ways. He saw that through her manipulation, she could do more harm than good so He took the manipulative woman out of the picture. I don't know about you but I want the Lord to bless me and keep me and not take me out of my life, my husband's life or my children's life. Somehow, some way I have to say BYE BYE manipulative spirit.

In reality, though, most women manipulate, some a little and some a lot. Most of us learn it as a young girl. We learn to manipulate our fathers, get them wrapped around our little fingers so we can get what we want from them. But fathers are different than husbands. Most fathers think it is cute when their little girl bats her eyes and begs for something. Or when a little girl says "But daddy, you promised and if you do this for me I will love you forever".

After the first year or so of marriage, batting your eyes and pouting your lips does not work. So you become a little more creative with your manipulation. You start using reverse psychology, "Oh no honey, that dress is way too expensive, I just don't deserve it...that is why I did not buy it". Your husband of 3 or less years will probably go out and get it for you because he wants you to believe you are worth it to him. HA HA you got him again.

But that manipulation technique does not last for long (men are smarter than we think). So now we get down and dirty and we even use sex as a manipulation tool. I have known women to withhold sex from their husband until they get what they want. These women are much braver than I am. I could not do that to my husband. I have read in multiple marriage books that sex for a man is very high up there on the need scale. For women it may be holding and touching but for men it is SEX.

When and if I use manipulation, I do it to get something I desperately need or desperately want. But I don't use manipulation to intentionally hurt my husband to get what I want.

Now sisters, by that last statement you probably think I think manipulation is ok to use. Well please hear me and hear my heart on this one. Manipulation is never the right thing or best thing to do to get what you want. Being open and honest and communicating directly will more likely get you what you want and what you need. But not only that, it is the mature and loving way to act in a relationship.

Sisters, it is time to take the focus off of you and put it on your partner. By meeting his needs and showing him love and support through open and honest communication, you are likely to never again have to manipulate him to get what you want. By putting the focus on him and meeting his needs, he will feel your love and devotion and most of all your respect for him. When a man feels respected, admired and loved, he will do just about anything for his partner…no manipulation required.

Blessings,

Debbie

Thoughts From The Word

For I know the plans I have for you," declares the Lord, "plans to prosper you and not to harm you, plans to give you hope and a future.

JEREMIAH 29:11

Sister,

How many times do we let our plans supersede what the Lord is telling us? We think we know better than God. Or like a fool, we shut Him out and don't follow His path and we go on our own journey to never never land. This passage in Jeremiah is quite clear, don't you think?

He has our plan. He knows where He wants to take us. God wants the very best for us. He will always look out for us and give us all we need to succeed down His path. His plan gives us hope and protection. Our plan leaves us wandering in the wilderness.

Thoughts From My Heart

CHRIST IN YOUR HOME

February 2011

Dear Sisters,

A year or so ago I wrote a statement in my little notebook that said, treat your husband how Christ would treat him if He was living in your house. Sometimes I regret writing that statement. You see, I read through my little note card book a couple times a month. It usually gives me encouragement or helps put me back on track spiritually and emotionally.

How every time I get to this statement, a cold chill runs down my spine and I get a little nauseated feeling in the pit of my stomach. I think to myself, can I really ever do this? Let me explain...I do treat my husband kindly and I do what ever I can to make his life easier as well as what ever I can do to make him happy. But I can't say I treat him the way Christ would. Now I don't think Jesus would necessarily cook and clean for him (but I guess you never know) but I do know Jesus would be more patient with him, would be more compassionate with him and above all would not think the thoughts I sometimes think about him. Let's be for real here, unless you are sister the saint, your thoughts are not always going to be loving, kind, compassionate and of good will for your spouse.

There may even be days, weeks or months that go by where you may not even like your husband but even during that time, Jesus will not stop loving your spouse nor will He stop loving you.

So how exactly would Christ treat your husband if He physically lived in the same house as you? I think it is pretty much summed up in 1 Corinthians 13: 4-7, 13 -4 *Love is patient, love is kind. It does not envy, it does not boast, it is not proud. 5 It does not dishonor others, it is not self-seeking, it is not easily angered, it keeps no record of wrongs. 6 Love does not delight in evil but rejoices with the truth. 7 It always protects, always trusts, always hopes, always perseveres. 13 And now these three remain: faith, hope and love. But the greatest of these is love.*

Let's examine this scripture. Love is patient: Love does not put a time line or a time constraint on someone. Love gives someone enough time and space for that person to grown and change. When love is patient, it allows others to make mistakes over and over again.

Love is kind and not jealous: Love rejoices when others succeed. Love treats others with care and compassion even when they may not deserve the care and compassion. Love does not desire what someone else has. Love does not allow for competition between people but allows for cheering on and sometimes the sheering up of others

Love does not brag and is not arrogant: Love does not allow you to talk badly of someone else while at the same time make yourself to be indestructible, never wrong and always needing to get your own way. Love does not allow you make yourself out to be better than everyone else.

Love does not act unbecomingly; it does not seek its own gratification but rather seeks the interests of others. Love does not allow you to go out there and do whatever you want, whatever feels good. Love makes sure you act appropriately so that you are not pulling your spouse down with you.

Love is not provoked. Love does not allow manipulation to come into a relationship to be used for selfish reason. And manipulation is always selfish. When you have love, no matter what that other person does, it will not provoke you to act against them

Love does not take in a wrong suffering. Love does not allow you to hold a grudge. No matter what the offense was from the person you love, love makes you forgive them. Love takes away any bitterness you may have for that person. Love truly allows you to forgive and forget. If you don't forgive and forget, the bitterness could kill your love and hence your relationship.

Love does not rejoice in unrighteousness but rejoices with the truth. Love does not gloss over things that are going to be hurtful. True love originates from the truth. Love allows you to tell someone their breath smells, they have gained a few pounds or that how they are treating you has really hurt you.

Love bears all things, believes all things, hopes all things and endures all things. Love will always hold any weight that a relationship can bring. Love will face every doubt that may be in relationship or doubt about yourself or doubt about your spouse. Love will always persist through hopelessness and love will last through any trial. Love does not leave when the going gets tough.

Love never fails. If love were to fail, then it would not be love.

Faith, Hope and Love …abide these three. But the greatest of these is love. Faith one day may not be needed because when we are in heaven we will see God and there will be no more need for faith. We hope for many things but one day everything we hoped for will be fulfilled. But love, there is no end.

So I suppose I answered my own question. How Jesus would treat my husband if He lived in our house? Jesus would never forget that love bears all things. Jesus would remember that my husband is human, just a man, a sinner who no matter how hard he tries, will never be perfect and without sin. But Jesus will never give up on him no matter what my husband's transgressions are, so Jesus expects me to never give up either. Thank you Jesus and I welcome Your love in my house.

Blessings,

Debbie

Thoughts From The Word

KEEP YOUR LIVES FREE FROM THE LOVE OF MONEY AND BE CONTENT WITH WHAT YOU HAVE BECAUSE GOD HAS SAID," NEVER WILL I LEAVE YOU; NEVER WILL I FORSAKE YOU" SO SAY WITH CONFIDENCE, "THE LORD IS MY HELPER, I WILL NOT BE AFRAID. WHAT CAN MAN DO TO ME"?

Hebrews 13: 5-6

Sister,
We all know money is an important part of living this life. Some of us are rolling in the dough will others are barely able to live paycheck to paycheck. Money buys us what we need and if we are fortunate enough money can also buy us what we want.

So if you are one of the millions of people who have very little tangible things, be content with that for right now. Thank God for the three shirts, two pair of pants and pair of shoes you have. The clothes may not be Chanel and the shoes may not be Jimmy Choo but you have some clothes to wear. Thank God.

As long as you have your faith in God, you will always have something. Don't be afraid of what tomorrow holds for you. Your relationship with the Lord will help you through. People may leave you and forsake you. You may even want to quite yourself, BUT God is your helper and He will never leave you.

Now if you are one of the sisters who has a closet full of designer clothes and you have more shoes than you can count, be cautious of putting too much stock in these material items. God wants you to put your confidence in Him. He wants you to remember that the only reason you got all of those things is because He allowed it. And because He allowed it, He can also take it away. Be content and know that God is always with you.

Thoughts From My Heart

INCREASE YOUR SELF-ACCEPTANCE

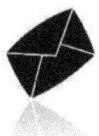

April 2011

Dear Sister,

Increase your self-acceptance and your opinion of yourself. Decide right now that not one more negative thing will ever come out of your mouth. The devil wants to bombard us with negative thoughts of our self so we will return to that pattern of thinking most of us learned growing up.

Be sober-minded; be watchful. Your adversary the devil prowls around like a roaring lion, seeking someone to devour. (1 Peter 5:8.) 2 Corinthians 11:3 - *"But I am afraid that just as Eve was deceived by the serpent's cunning, your minds may somehow be led astray from your sincere and pure devotion to Christ."*

When I want to do good, evil is right there with me. -For in my inner being I delight in God's law; but I see another law at work in the members of my body, waging war against the law of my mind and making me a prisoner of the law of sin at work within my members. (Romans 7:21-23)

Wow, negative thoughts can sure overtake our minds. From reading these scriptures, negative thoughts and lack of self-acceptance has been going on for thousands of years. I don't know about you sister, but I grew up in a pretty negative house. Nothing I ever did seemed to be good enough and/or I never did anything right.

What was even more confusing was if you did get a compliment there was usually a backhanded negative comment that came right after. I also got blamed for a lot of things, things I did not even do.

I remember many a times I would be upstairs in my room and my mom would drop something in the kitchen and she would scream up to me, "See what you made me do Deborah!" I would be like Mom, "I was not even downstairs" and she would say "Well I was thinking about how you didn't (you name it could have been anything) and you made me drop this."

Even when I moved away and went to college, the negative thoughts about me still followed. For many, many years I let these thoughts influence many aspects of my life. Anything that I accomplished was still never good enough in my eyes. Negative thoughts, especially about me consumed my mind. When you do not think very highly of your self or your accomplishments, you tend to take everything that some says as a personal attack against you.

Someone could tell you how someone else did something nice for them, maybe for their birthday or maybe just because and your thoughts automatically go to "wow, I should have done that. Gosh my gift really did not matter to them. See I just can never seem to get it right."

My, my, just by writing this statement, I feel the hair on the back of my neck standing up. It is an awful feeling to constantly be in competition with others as well as in competition with yourself. And why all this competition? Simply because you feel you have to outdo everyone else and you even have to outdo yourself. Talk about stress and internal chaos.

Someone who you don't even respect may come up to you and tell you that they don't like that color on you or that they are not crazy about your new hair cut. If you are a negative person, you will automatically take those words as an attack on you as a person. You will get mad, sulk and withdraw as well as you will probably go home and change your outfit and contemplate how soon you can get your hair color changed. The real interesting thing about this is that this comment came from someone you don't even respect. Just imagine what would happen to you if such comments came from someone you love and cared about. Oh my.

So here you are at this time in your life and you still have negative thoughts and because of these thoughts you feel unworthy. You feel unworthy of love, unworthy of the accomplishments that you achieved, unworthy of the possessions that you have, even unworthy of God's unconditional love. Now what?

I started off this letter to you sister to not let one more negative word come out of your mouth and I also said to not let the devil bombard your thought process with negative thinking, right? So here is my humble advice. Daily and I mean daily, you are going to have to

recognize each and every negative word that comes out of your mouth and you are going to have to ask God to give you new words to use to replace these words.
You are also going to have to seek Gods forgiveness daily and maybe even multiple times a day about the words you use. You are going to have to want this so bad because if you have had negative words spewing out of your mouth for years, just know this may not change for you instantly.

You also can not allow the devil to infiltrate your mind with negativism, unworthiness, loneliness and rejection. When one of those thoughts comes into your mind, you must abolish it. You have to recognize it and then you have to want to put in the effort to change the though and change the perspective. I work at this daily and I am nowhere near perfecting it. When all of your life you may have heard things like "Glad you won this time but just remember you are only as good as your last win" or something as simple as, "Why are you eating that, don't you know that it will just make you fatter."

I don't know what happens in your mind but I know what happens in my mind, "Gosh, I got to work even harder to win again next time," and "Wow, they are saying I am fat. Well, I might as well keep eating it, I am already fat and there is nothing I can do." So this shows that you are constantly competing with yourself and never being good enough and feeling bad about yourself and doing things that are viewed as self-destructive.

Sister, work hard at getting these thoughts out of your mind no matter what anyone tells you. When these

thoughts are allowed to accumulate and you also let your feelings get involved you will spin in a downward cycle that is hard to get out of. Your mind is actually in hell and the devil is enjoying his playtime on the swings and slides of your mind.
Don't go there. Don't let the devil run free.

God made you worthy by dying on the cross for you and forgiving all of your sins. Believe it or not, you would never have to win another competition, you would not have to have the cleanest house on the block or the most perfect kids or the bestest husband. You don't need to cook the most awesome meal for a dinner party of 30 or have shoes that feel good and match every outfit. God finds you worthy. He made you worthy.

When I had a few quiet minutes with God the other day, I was once again feeling unworthy and just was allowing those negative lonely feelings enter my heart. God said to me that even when you are ungrateful for all that I have done for you and through you; I love you so much that I still do not find you unworthy.

 Sister, don't you realize that when we have negative thoughts and we feel all of those things about ourselves we are really slapping God in the face. Yep, we are. We know that the Lord suffered a horrific death and rose from the dead and because you believe in Him you have a place in heaven. However then we allow the devil to stir up our minds and manipulate our tongues and think and feel basically ungrateful. Negative thoughts and reactions show ingratitude for all He has done for you.

It is what it is. Sister let's ask the Lord every day to take over our thoughts and our words and let's decide right now to not let one more negative word to come out of our mouth or allow these thoughts to bombard our mind.

Be Blessed,

Debbie

Thoughts From The Word

So do not worry or be anxious about tomorrow, for tomorrow will have worries and anxieties of its own. Sufficient for each day is its own trouble.

Matthew 6:34

Sister,

In my past I have been a chronic worrier. I worried about what was going to happen the next hour let alone the next day, week or month. I really like to have things planned out and when plans change my anxiety level goes through the roof.

I say it is because I like to always be in the know. Others may say it is because I am a control freak. I realized my constant worrying was a problem when we planned a trip to Jamaica. I had heard that the streets we very tight and winding and the bus that we would have to take from the airport to the hotel, which was two hours away, went very fast down these tight windy roads. I had also heard that there were quite a few bus accidents because of this.

So as soon as the trip was planned, I started to worry that the bus we would be driving on would tip over. So three months before the trip, I had my escape route all planned out for when the bus tipped over. I spent those three months worrying about something I had no control over. Because of my worry, I missed out on the excitement of planning the trip with my family and when we arrived in Jamaica, I missed out on all the beauty during the bus ride. I was just waiting on the bus to flip over so I could put my plan into action.

Needless to say, the bus did not tip over and we arrived at our destination unscathed. So for months and months, I wasted energy, planning and anticipating disaster.

I think back on that worry and many other worries and I now realize what a waste of time and energy. I have come to understand that even living a Christian life, each day can bring potential trouble, but I can't waste my time worrying about it or getting myself so upset and anxious that I feel physically sick. I now just call on Jesus's name and He relieves my anxiety. He's got it in control.

Thoughts From My Heart

DO NOT ALLOW THE WAY OTHER PEOPLE TREAT YOU TO DETERMINE YOUR VALUE.

June 2011

Sister,

There are so many days I feel of little value to anyone including myself. Why is this? I let other peoples harsh words and what people think about me determine how I will think and feel about myself for that day. But God, **"You are my refuge and my shield; I have put my hope in your word. Away from me, you evildoers, that I may keep the commands of my God!"** (Psalms119:114-115). I have to constantly remind myself to not view myself as others view me, but view myself as God wants me to be.

If we get caught up in what value others have placed on us, we will never fulfill Gods plan for our life. For most of my life, I tried to please people (which I have determined is impossible). I would go out of my way to do special things for them or take on projects no one else wanted just so they might treat me better and acknowledge me. I wanted them to value me and value my hard work and effort. They may appreciate what I had done at that time and valued my contribution, but it was usually fleeting.

In my last job as a hospital executive, I was never ever celebrated by my peers. Gosh, I was barely tolerated. I worked with basically the same people for the seven years I was there and they never treated me like I had value. You are probably thinking, then why the heck would you stay? I stayed because the Lord told me to stay. You see I may not have been valued by my peers but the people who reported to me and who I worked closely with did value me as a person and they valued the work that I accomplished.

During the seven years I was there, I learned a lot about myself and I gained insight into various personalities. But most of all I learned a great deal about God and what He values. **"It was good for me to be afflicted so that I might learn your decrees."** (Psalm 119:71).

During the time I was employed at this hospital, I had to pray morning, noon and night. I had to pray on my way to work to get up enough boldness to even walk through the doors because I knew as soon as I entered I would be under heavy spiritual attack. I prayed and read a couple of bible verses and affirmations when I got into my office so that my office would be a "safe place". I prayed before I meet with one of my peers, I prayed after meeting with one of my peers (mostly for forgiveness since they tended to bring out the worst in me) and I prayed on the way home for my head to be cleared of all of the negativity, self-doubt and criticism.

Many of days I got great comfort from the Lord and I was able to have a good attitude and I was able to feel peaceful. However, when you are devalued every day and for many hours during the day, the devil can sure have his way with you. You start to begin to believe what people are saying about you. You begin to expect to be treated poorly and to be disrespected. This poison gets into your spirit and begins to destroy everything you once were and everything you know yourself to be. You feel yourself going down this slippery slope and you are reaching for a rope to help pull you back up. You know the rope is there, your fingertips touch it but you can't seem to get a grasp.

During this time, I often felt that way. I knew the rope was there (God) I even was able to touch it throughout the day (by praying and seeking Him) but for some reason, I could never fully grasp a hold of the rope to keep me pulled up on top of the mountain. The reason…I let other people determine my value instead of listening to what God had to say about me. *"Peace I leave with you; my peace I give you. I do not give to you as the world gives. Do not let your hearts be troubled and do not be afraid."* (John 14:27)

There may be times you don't even feel valued in your home by the ones who are supposed to love you and of course value and respect you. Feeling unvalued or undervalued by the ones you love actually hurts much worse than being undervalued by people you work with or people you socialize with.

You might feel taken for granted around the house, ya know, "leave the dishes mom will do it" or "Gosh baby the whites did not come out very clean, can you wash them again?" or "Thanks for dinner but I am not going to eat right now I have too much work to do", or "Hey why are you so tired all of the time"...I could go on and I am sure you could too.

I do believe that the devil uses the people you love the most to destroy your relationship with God. We expect criticism from non-family members, we expect attacks on our character but we don't expect them from the people we love the most. We expect their unconditional support and concern but we rarely get it.
"I have set the LORD always before me. Because he is at my right hand, I will not be shaken".
(Psalm 16:8.)

We need to know who and what we are in Gods eyes. *"For we are God's workmanship, created in Christ Jesus to do good works, which God prepared in advance for us to do"* (Ephesians 2:1).

Seek God to find your value here on earth and your eternal value in heaven. When you are able to do this, it does not matter how anyone treats you. Your value was determined before you were born and when Jesus died for us; your value was sealed forever. Don't let people rent space in your head. Allow Jesus to live in there because He already paid the price.

Blessings,
Debbie

Thoughts From The Word

CREATE IN ME A PURE HEART, O GOD, AND RENEW A STEADFAST SPIRIT WITHIN ME.

PSALM 51:10

A pure heart does not judge
A pure heart loves
A pure heart forgives
A pure heart shows patience
A pure heart shows understanding
A pure heart is not controlled by the mind
A pure heart guards itself
A pure heart exhibits wisdom

When you have a pure heart, God will dwell within you and give you patience and make you resolute in what you believe. By having a pure heart, the Lord will make you trustworthy and dependable.

Thoughts From My Heart

NO FEAR HERE

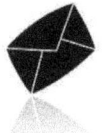

October 24, 2011

Dear Sister,

I am writing you this letter during a season of the year that is normally associated with scary movies, scary costumes and scary stomach aches. When we watch something scary, we can allow our mind to play tricks on us and cause us to be too fearful to go into our closets, turn out the lights and even to fall asleep.

My husband, even though he is an incredibly saved Christian, loves scary movies. Not really the gory ones but the psychological thrillers that make your mind go in all different directions.

I, on the other hand, hated all scary movies. When I did watch them, I would have nightmares. I remember one night being at the movie theater with my boyfriend at the time. We were watching the original Halloween. I was squeezing his hand so hard the whole time we were in the theater.

If you have never seen the movie, close to the end of the movie, there is a scene where the bad guy/killer Michael

Meyer, falls out of a window. When they first show you the ground, he is there all sprawled out. Well, when that happened, I released the death grip I had on my boyfriend's hand and breathed a sigh of relief.

But 30 seconds later, they showed the ground again, and Michael Meyer was not there. Well, I lost it. I let out a huge scream and covered my face and jumped on my boyfriend's lap.

Well actually, I did not jump on his lap; I jumped on the man's lap next to me. I was screaming and making an absolute scene. He tapped me on the shoulder and then I realized what I had done. Boy oh boy did I feel ridiculous for letting this movie affect me like it did.

To top the night off, when I got home, I woke my dad up and made him go look in my closet to make sure no one was in there as well as I made him look under my bed. That night my dad forbid me to see scary movies again. Who could blame him. However obedience is not my strong point.

So over the years, I have watched many, many scary movies, especially since I have gotten married to my husband. But you know what? They don't scare me as much as they used to. The fear and anxiety that would well up inside me barley makes my pulse increase anymore.

I started thinking, why is that? The movies today are actually scarier than they used to be so why has my fear subsided? Simply stated it is maturity. I used to be fearful that those terrible things would happen to me.

When I was younger, I had an unhealthy fear of God. I thought He would allow bad things to happen to me, to get me back for the bad things that I had done. I thought He would do this even if I asked for forgiveness and repented, you know say the 10 Hail Mary's and 10 Our Fathers.

Through my continuing journey with God, I have come to realize that fear is not alright in any amount. Fear is not natural and God did not create fear. God created peace and love. Fear is not ok and we cannot operate in fear and be successful.

"For I know the plans that I have for you declares the Lord. Plans for welfare and not for calamity to give you a future and a hope." (Jeremiah 29:11)

"So do not worry or be anxious about tomorrow, for tomorrow will have worries and anxieties of its own. Sufficient for each day is its own trouble." (Mathew 6:34.)

"Be not afraid or dismayed at this great multitude, foir the battle is not yours but Gods... You shall not need to fight in this battle; take you positions, stand still and see the deliverance of the Lord." (2 Chronicles 20: 15 and 17)

"In addition to all of this, take up the shield of faith, with which you can extinguish all the flaming arrows of the evil one". (Ephesians 6:16)

"Faith and fear are directly opposite. Fear is contaminated faith. If you tolerate your fear you are contaminating your faith. For God did not give us a spirit of fear but of power, of love and a sound mind." (2 Timothy 1:7)   Fear and unbelief go hand in hand. Worry is fear based. This means you are mediating on the wrong things.

"Therefore I tell you do not worry about your life, what you will eat or drink or about your body. What you will wear. Is not life more important than food and the body more important than clothes? Look at the birds in the air, they do not sow or reap or store away in barns, and yet your heavenly Father feeds them. Are you not much more valuable than they? Who of you by worrying add a single hour to your life." (Matthew 6: 25-27)

Take authority over fear with words. It may help if you memorize one of the scripture from above and hear yourself say it out loud. Fear cannot rule in my life anymore because I have favor with God and I will not worry about the crazy things I used to think of.

Your mind is oh so very powerful. What you meditate on and think about constantly can actually become truth in your life. Don't let your mind keep going back to the situations or circumstances in your life that made you afraid and that made you worry. You really need to believe that God is in control. You are wasting your time and energy thinking about those things that cause fear.

Think about the following to help you rid yourself of fear:
- I will not allow fear and worry to overtake me because worry and fear can block my blessings.
- Worry is fear based and it comes from meditating on the wrong things.
- Fear and unbelief go hand in hand because if you believe in God, God will not allow fear to enter your life.
- Fear is not natural. God did not create fear.
- Fear is NOT ok and we will not operate in it.

I still can become frightened at times. A loud noise, an unexpected clap of thunder can quickly frighten me. A diagnosis of a disease in my body, or concern about how all the bills will be paid can also still cause me temporary worry or fear. But I have faith and trust in God that He only wants to prosper me, He only wants to heal me and He only wants to comfort me when I am afraid of even the smallest thing. With this faith and trust comes peace of mind, body and soul.

Just remember sister, the world tries to scar you and keep your mind oppressed each and every day. The world wants you to live in fear and to worry constantly. The world scares you with what is on TV and in the movies. The world tries to scare you with what comes in your mailbox. The world tries to scare you with bad reports from the Dr's office. The world tries to scare you with bad reports for your child's teachers. The world tries to scare you with the word recession, losing your home and not having money to feed your family.

Remember, God did not create fear. The world created fear. Have faith and trust in God's word and Gods promise to you and **Fear Not**.

Blessings,

Debbie

Letters to My Sister

www.ingramcontent.com/pod-product-compliance
Lightning Source LLC
Chambersburg PA
CBHW032124090426
42743CB00007B/457